Help Me Find My Painting!

Cindy Prince

Book 3: Eugène Delecroix

Hi there!

My name is Tigre.

One minute, I was chasing a snake, and the next? I was here!

If I give you clues...

Will you help me find my painting?

Delecroix loved painting emotions, and many Romantic painters used wild animals to give freedom to their deepest - and sometimes scariest - feelings.

Finding our painting is going to be tricky.

Look closely at my face.

Do you see how wild and ferocious it is?

Now look at the movement of my tail.

Does this look exactly like a realistic tail?

What do these loose brush strokes make you see and feel?

My painting is meant to make you feel something!

Do you think you can
find it?

Let's Go!

Is this my painting?

A Painter's Studio

What do you think?

No!

Why not?

There are some bright colors, but the people in this painting don't look emotional at all.

Do you see how the brush strokes are precise to give this painting a realistic look?

Is this my painting?

Wivenhoe Park, Essex

What do you think?

No!

Why not?

It's a beautiful scene, but again, much too peaceful.

This is also a painting of a scene you could observe in real life!

Do you feel a strong emotion when you look at this painting?

Is this my painting?

Alpine Mastiffs Reanimating a Distressed Traveler.

What do you think?

No!

Why not?

This painting IS of animals, and it depicts an emotional scene.

But do you see how the brush strokes are still a little too careful?

We're getting closer...

Is this my painting?

The Trap

What do you think?

No!

Why not?

Now the brush strokes are a little *too* free!

Do you see how there aren't any details on the people's faces? This gives the *impression* of people.

What do you feel when you look at this scene?

Is this my painting?

Tiger and Snake

What do you think?

Yes!

Tiger and Snake

You helped me find my painting!

Christopher Columbus and His Son at La Rábida

Eugène Delacroix

He is considered the leading painter of the French Romantic movement.

He learned how to paint by copying the work of other master artists whose work was displayed in the Louvre museum.

Did you know he survived drowning, poisoning, choking, and a serious fire to then produce 9,000 artworks during his lifetime?

He loved to portray emotional scenes from literature, mythology, religion, and politics.

Romantic artists focused on emotion with less precise brushstrokes and color. Can you see that in the next two paintings?

Arabs Skirmishing in the Mountains

Two Studies of an Indian from Calcutta, Seated and Standing

Eugène Delacroix
French, 1798 - 1863

Eugène Delacroix was born in 1798, the son of Charles Delacroix who had served briefly as minister of foreign affairs under the Directory and who was on a mission to Holland, as the ambassador of the French Republic, at the time of his son's birth. His mother, Victoire Oeben, was descended from a family of artisans and craftsmen. Both parents died early, the father in 1805, the mother in 1814, leaving Eugène in the care of his older sister, Henriette de Verninac, wife of a former ambassador to Turkey and minister-plenipotentiary to Switzerland. The fall of Napoleon's empire spelled the temporary ruin of this family of high officials, and with it that of young Delacroix. But the influential relations among which his birth and childhood had placed him were to protect his subsequent career, particularly in those periods, after 1830 and again after 1850, when Bonapartist interests were on the rise. As a child he had played on the knees of Talleyrand, his father's successor in the Ministry of Foreign Affairs and a family friend. It has been suggested, but not proven, that Talleyrand, to whom Delacroix in later life bore a marked facial resemblance, was in fact his actual father.

In 1815 Delacroix, aged seventeen, began to take painting lessons from Pierre Guérin (1774-1833) through whose studio Théodore Gericault had briefly and turbulently passed a little earlier. Guérin was a tolerant teacher who attracted the sons of the middle class. His classicist instruction had little effect on Delacroix; it was less important for his development than the literary education that he had received at the lycée. The example of Gericault with whom he was acquainted and for whose Raft of the Medusa (Louvre) he posed in 1818 left its mark on him, but in every essential respect he was, like many of his contemporaries, a self-taught artist, whose real school was the Louvre, where, even after the removal of the Napoleonic loot, the splendor of Titian, Veronese, and Rubens shone brightly enough to eclipse the school of David. Among his fellow copyists in its galleries he met the young Englishman Richard Parkes Bonington (1801-1828) who, together with his friend Raymond Soulier, was to introduce him to watercolor painting and a British tradition of colorism, and who helped to awaken his interest in Shakespeare, Byron, and Scott, the main literary sources of his romanticism.

Delacroix' student work did not show extraordinary promise, but in 1822 his Salon debut, the Bark of Dante (Louvre), attracted some attention. Though it has a deserved place in the history of art, as the start of a great career, it is still an immature effort, heavy-handed in its combination of reminiscences of Gericault, Rubens, and Michelangelo, and incoherent in its composition. Two years later, his Massacres of Chios (Louvre) burst upon the Salon of 1824 as "a terrifying hymn in honor of doom and irremediable suffering" (Charles Baudelaire, "L'Oeuvre et la vie d'Eugène Delacroix," published as L'Art romantique, Paris, 1869). The picture's resonant harmonies gave an early indication of Delacroix' mastery of color, and its lustful stress on horror and death struck a note that was to sound throughout much of his subsequent work. The government's purchase of the work enabled Delacroix to visit England in the spring and summer of 1825. He had already seen landscapes by John Constable (1776-1837) in Paris while at work on Massacres of Chios. Further impressions of English art and literature gathered during his months in London were to influence him in the following years, as is evident in his Portrait of Baron Switer (1826, National Gallery, London), a bravura performance in the manner of Thomas Lawrence (1769-1830), and in his use of subjects from Scott and Byron. His Execution of the Doge Marino Faliero (1826, Wallace Collection, London), based on a play by Byron and painted with something of Bonington's nervous brilliance, is the crowning achievement of his English phase.

After these paintings of exquisite finish and relatively small format, the colossal, orgiastic Death of Sardanapalus (Louvre), shown at the Salon of 1827, came as a shock to the public. Delacroix had taken the subject from a play by Byron but supplied the voluptuous cast of this scene of slaughter from his own imagination. He paid for his audacity with a temporary loss of official favor. The following years were a difficult but productive period during which he experimented with a variety of subjects: studies of lions and tigers, oriental scenes, sensuous nudes, and turbulent battles.

The Revolution of 1830 inspired his one truly popular work, Liberty Leading the People (Louvre). In the place of the febrile romanticism of his paintings of the 1820s, he now used a larger, more sober manner and colors of muted intensity. Dealing with this modern subject he achieved poetic effect without morbidity or false grandeur: even Liberty, abundantly physical, has the effect of adding a note of actuality rather than allegorical artifice to the tumult on the barricade.

For once, public and critics united in praise of the artist, and the government of Louis-Philippe awarded him the Legion of Honor.

In early 1832 Delacroix visited North Africa in the suite of a French embassy to the sultan of Morocco. Islamic Africa surpassed all his expectations. The classical beauty for which he had vainly looked among the plaster casts in Guérin's studio he now encountered along roadsides under the African sky. He filled sketchbooks with observations of Arab life and gathered a store of ideas that served him for the rest of his life. On his return to Paris, he began a series of oriental subjects, not Byronic fantasies now but recollections of actual experience. Algerian Women in Their Apartment (1834, Louvre) records his recollection of a visit to a harem with the quiet authority of fact rather than the fictions of romantic exoticism. The sensuous intensity of the painting results from stylistic means that seem simpler but are in fact more complex than those that produced the sensational Sardanapalus. It signals the attainment of his mature style, quieter but grander than his earlier manner, more monumental yet no less expressive, more restrained but more powerful.

Early in his career, Delacroix had been hailed by the young French romantics as their leader. During the 1830s he outgrew this affiliation, not because he had changed his course, but because his fellow romantics were failing to keep up with him. The "romantic battle" had been won too easily. After 1830 French romanticism became popular and died. Its followers, agreeable but minor talents for the most part, rapidly declined into picturesqueness and mannerism. Delacroix, by contrast, increasingly identified himself with the grand traditions of the Venetians and Flemings, with

Veronese and Rubens above all. His later works expressed a growing concern with traditional subject matter and monumental form. In his Entry of the Crusaders into Constantinople (Louvre), shown at the Salon of 1840, he resumed compositional devices that he had used earlier in Massacres of Chios, but the former violence is stilled by the somber harmony of the colors and the weight of the great colonnade that dominates the scene. In his Justice of Trajan (Musée des Beaux-Arts, Rouen) shown at the same Salon, an even more elaborate architectural setting contains, with its strong verticals and diagonals, the animation of the figures.

Behind Delacroix' new concern with compositional structure and balance lay the experience he had gained in carrying out the architectural decorations that occupied him during the latter part of his life. The governments of Louis-Philippe and Napoleon III favored him with important monumental commissions, beginning in 1833 with the allegorical decorations of the Salon du Roi in the Palais Bourbon (Chamber of Deputies). This was closely followed by the even larger enterprise of the Palais Bourbon's library (1838-1847), where Delacroix covered a succession of domes and pendentives with scenes celebrating the heroic lineage of the arts and sciences, in a dramatic succession beginning with Orpheus' gift of civilization to mankind and ending with Attila's destruction of Italy. Before this was finished, he received the further commission of decorating the library of the Senate in the Luxembourg Palace (1840-1846), where, in the central dome, he painted the presentation of Dante to Homer and the other great men of Greek and Roman antiquity, to symbolize the meeting of the classical pagan with the modern Christian culture. There followed the ceiling of the Galerie d'Apollon in the Louvre (1850-1851), the decorations in the Salon de la Paix of the Hôtel de Ville of Paris (1852-1854, destroyed in 1871), and the Chapel of the Holy Angels in the church of Saint-Sulpice (1854-1861). No other painter of the time was so continuously employed in monumental work on the grandest scale, none was given such opportunities to triumph in public on ceilings, domes, and walls. His superiority rested in part on his mastery of color that provided both the emotional force and the formal structure of his murals. He was the most versatile of the painters of his time, including in the range of his subjects battlefield and barricade, Faust and Hamlet, royal tiger and odalisque.

The Universal Exposition in 1855 showed thirty-six of his paintings, a tribute to him (together with Ingres) as one of France's two preeminent living artists. Having long been denied admission to the Academy, of which he privately took a coolly realistic view, he was at last admitted to this body of distinguished mediocrities in 1857. Frequently ill with bronchial infections and economizing his physical strength, he lived a frugal bachelor's life but worked with unabated energy until the end. For all his courtesy, his person could command awe and, on occasion, a secret terror. In one of his last works, the National Gallery's Arabs Skirmishing in the Mountains (1966.12.1), he remembered once more his African voyage, the great adventure of his early years. He died, not long after completing this painting, on 13 August 1863.
--*The National Gallery of Art*

Art Citations

Boilly, Louis-Léopold. A Painter's Studio. c.1800.
    Chester Dale Collection. National Gallery of Art.
    https://www.nga.gov/collection/art-object-page.12199.html

Constable, John. Wivenhoe Park, Essex. 1816.
    Widener Collection. National Gallery of Art.
    https://www.nga.gov/collection/art-object-page.1147.html

Lanser, Sir Edwin Lanser. Alpine Mastiffs Reanimating a Distressed Traveler. 1820.
    Patron's Permanent Fund. National Gallery of Art.
    https://www.nga.gov/collection/art-object-page.220510.html

de Toulouse-Loutrec, Paul. The Trap. 1880.
    Collection of Mr. and Mrs. Paul Mellon. National Gallery of Art.
    https://www.nga.gov/collection/art-object-page.89686.html

Delacroix, Eugène. Arabs Skirmishing in the Mountains. c. 1863.
    Chester Dale Fund. National Gallery of Art.
    https://www.nga.gov/collection/art-object-page.50686.html

Delacroix, Eugène. Two Studies of an Indian from Calcutta, Seated and Standing. c.1823/24
    Collection of Mr. and Mrs. Paul Mellon. National Gallery of Art.
    https://www.nga.gov/collection/art-object-page.136016.html

Delacroix, Eugène. Christopher Columbus and His Son at La Rábida. 1838.
    Chester Dale Collection. National Gallery of Art.
    https://www.nga.gov/collection/art-object-page.46602.html

Delacroix, Eugène. Tiger and Snake. 1862.
    Corcoran Collection (William A. Clark Collection). National Gallery of Art.
    https://www.nga.gov/collection/art-object-page.195132.html

About the Author

Cindy is first and foremost mother to her four beautiful children and wife to her charming and handsome husband, Scott. She is a musician, a gardener, an athlete, an actor, a lover of Canadian chocolate, and most recently, a writer.

Cindy grew up in Airdrie, AB, Canada, but has lived most of her adult life between California and Colorado. She currently resides in the Denver metro area. Cindy graduated from Brigham Young University in 2005 with a B.S. in Psychology, minoring in Business. She serves actively within her church and community and is always up for a new adventure.

After homeschooling for nine years and having countless discussions with her own four children, Cindy decided to start taking notes. Her picture books are inspired by real conversation and interests with the goal of providing stories that are both fun and helpful for families like her own.

@CindyGWrites
www.CindyPrinceAuthor.com

Made in the USA
Coppell, TX
26 May 2022